THE ROOTS OF DEVELOPING
AGRICULTURE IN THE
SOUTH AFRICAN CONTEXT

THE ROOTS OF DEVELOPING
AGRICULTURE IN THE
SOUTH AFRICAN CONTEXT

MCGREGGOR S. NTULI

authorHOUSE®

AuthorHouse™ UK Ltd.
1663 Liberty Drive
Bloomington, IN 47403 USA
www.authorhouse.co.uk
Phone: 0800.197.4150

Published by AuthorHouse 01/20/2014

ISBN: 978-1-4918-8705-9 (sc)
ISBN: 978-1-4918-8706-6 (e)

CONTENTS

ACKNOWLEDGEMENTS

I would like to express my sincere gratitude to many people who saw me through this book; to all those who provided support, talked things over, read, wrote, offered comments and assisted in the editing, proofreading and design.

Additional and special acknowledgements go to the following people for their various efforts, contributions and inspiration, without which this book wouldn't have been written.

  I. My mom, Zodwa for making this book a success in every way
  II. My brother, Thulani for his encouragement and typing
  III. My spouse, Tina for giving me courage and believing in me
  IV. Kgomotso Sehoole for proofreading
  V. Khathutshelo Neluheni for editing, proofreading and for sharing his knowledge and expertise on the subject matter
  VI. Author house for making it possible for me to publish this book

Lastly I'll give credit to all of those who have been with me over the years of my career.

DEDICATIONS

This book is dearly dedicated to my daughter, Tshegofatso who stimulates the best in me, my mom (Zodwa) for her guidance, upbringing and making me the person I am. Finally, to everyone who commits themselves in contributing towards the well-being of the agricultural industry of South Africa.

DISCLAIMER

The content of this book reflects the views of the author which are based mainly on his experiences and expertise on the subject. Much emphasis is deliberately placed on the norms and experiences that take place at the operational level of the industry as opposed to elaborating on literature based findings or documented strategies that do not reflect the actual circumstances. The subject matter is not intended to address the pros and cons of the entire scope of the industry, but it's meant to focus specifically on the common issues that are experienced primarily by developing farmers and to a lesser extent the servants of the South African agricultural industry. As a result of this, most data and information has been acquired informally (without the use of a formalised questionnaire) through prearranged farmer visits, by training developing farmers, exchanging views with role players of the industry and by attending various agricultural functions that place emphasis on topics that are similar to that of the book. Due to unforeseen dynamics of change, some views expressed in this book could change with time without any notice. Finally, the author declares no intentions of negative perception or conflict to any person who is affected by this subject.

PREFACE

In the current era of the modernised South Africa, it may be quite difficult or even almost impossible to raise an issue that relates to the transformation of human livelihoods without creating a political or racial implication. This fact is largely (if not totally) due to the political history of this country. Although historic events are usually used as points of reference when unfolding a subject that deals with the creation of equal opportunities, they are not always intended to cause any commotion amongst its citizens, but rather should be viewed as a source of measuring the progress of equality.

However, without dwelling much on political connotations or creating perceptions of any racial implications to any ethnical group what so ever, this book seeks to put the current status and possible future position of the South African agricultural sector (particularly Developing Agriculture) into perspective. Amongst other things, this will be done by clearly defining the types of farmers that the industry is trying to empower. After all, the empowering of developing farmers is one of the major intentions of this industry. Hence defining and distinguishing the different levels of farming would be of vital importance due to the fact that some agriculturalists who are involved in empowering these farmers have little knowledge on the types of farmers they are actually serving.

Experience has shown that a large proportion of these agriculturalists battle to understand the farmers' position in terms of the resources that are most commonly required by them, the type of assistance they need in order to ensure that they obtain basic resources, the support structure that would ascertain their growth and development, as well as their frustrations that are brought upon by the conditions that are often made prerequisites of accessing relevant assistance. If the actual position of such farmers is not clearly understood by the servants of their industry, then it creates the room for them to be rendered with ineffective services in a snow balling effect. For reasons such as the above, this book could be used as one of the building blocks that are required to establish the common grounds of Developing Agriculture in addition to it being used as a guidance tool for steering the industry into what is regarded to be the right direction. The right direction is one that will enhance the progress made in Developing Agriculture. Some of the other building blocks will obviously include publications from the public and private sectors, as well as all sorts of formal and informal gatherings between officials and farmers.

By virtue of the identified challenge stated above, the primary aim of the book is to determine the major components that would constitute a successfully progressive agricultural industry given the transition that it's currently undergoing. This will be done by simply highlighting on what is viewed as the critical goal/s of this industry, the challenges associated with it, as well as the possible solutions that may be required to achieve the goal/s of the industry. It's not as if these components are not entirely known to many of us, it's just that they aren't clearly understood or properly consolidated in one comprehensive manuscript. Some of the information documented in this book has been informally gathered by combining valuable opinions that are often expressed by various role players who make different contributions in the industry.

Following the observations of the shortfalls associated with the industry, the urge of putting these findings in writing came into being. This clearly illustrates that writing this book came as a result of a self-determined task that was established after realising that various agriculturalists, institutions and other role players who are involved in Developing Agriculture have often expressed different perspectives with regards to the most appropriate winning formula that needs to be applied to ensure the ultimate success of refining the industry (which is also one of the reasons why there's a need for continuous gatherings and publishing). To put this in a different context, everyone involved in refining this valuable industry sings the same song regarding its future well-being, but the major difference is that they sing it in different tunes. This therefore creates a negative impact on the harmony of the song that is sung by the industry.

However, it needs to be emphasized that this book is not intended to cover any technical agricultural content since it (the technical information) does not constitute the core content of the book. Besides, such information is sufficiently published within the South African agricultural context. This simply implies that, if and when distributed correctly, technical information is always readily available to developing farmers in abundance. It is brought to them in the form of print media, various published articles and posters, television programs, extension services, farmers/information days, private consultations as well as other formal gatherings. Providing this information in such diverse forms enhances the maximum uptake of it amongst developing farmers regardless of their literacy level.

Thus, the contents will unfold on the seed/s that need to be planted, as well as the methods of nurturing it in order to ensure that South Africans have an industry that will flourish rapidly and fruitfully. To put this statement in its simplest form, the content is meant to cover the most basic elements that need to be considered in developing the industry. Hence the topic: The Roots of Developing Agriculture In The South African Context.

1

INTRODUCTORY POINTS TO NOTE: THE HISTORY AND IMPACT OF AGRICULTURE IN SOUTH AFRICA

A brief overview of the South African history

As clichéd as it may sound, it is a generally known fact that the dawn of the year 1994 marked the beginning of a new era in the history of South Africa. This year gave birth to what was since then regarded as the "New South Africa". This meant that most if not all norms, practices and priorities of the country would change. Amongst other things, it's the inequality that was brought upon by the previous governance that was to be changed. It is the same inequality that created oppressive laws and restrictions that clearly divided the nation in terms of its social activities, geographical positioning, educational systems and career paths amongst other things. Thus a clear distinction of supremacy and inferiority between citizens was established.

Remedying the unpleasant history

In order for the prescribed change to occur, some of the economic, social and cultural norms of the previous era had to be transformed. It is therefore from this transformation process that equal opportunities for all would be promoted by simply eliminating the restrictions that were created back then. As a result of this transformation process, all ordinary citizens have been granted the freedom to develop themselves through participating in any legal activity that would not only improve their livelihoods, but that will also contribute towards the economic development of a new era in a supposedly "new country".

Given all the above stated connotations, the agricultural industry has been identified as one of the contributors of developing the economy of the "New South Africa".

What impact does agriculture have on the economy of this developing country?

Although it has been neglected and incorrectly perceived by some citizens in the past, it is commonly known to many of us by now that the agricultural industry is one of the sectors that have both a direct and an indirect influence on the South African economy. According to the *South African Government Information, 2012*, primary agriculture contributes about 3% of South Africa's gross domestic product (GDP) and 7% of formal employment as its direct contribution to the economy. Furthermore, it is estimated that there are around 8.5 million people who directly or indirectly depend on agriculture for their employment and income (*South Africa.info. South African Agriculture. 2012*). In addition to this, many of the other sectors that contribute towards the development of the local economy depend on agriculture for the supply of raw materials and/or resources. The textile industry is an excellent example of such dependents of agriculture. This makes it evidently clear that it is undoubtedly one of the pillars of the local economy. Subsequent to this fact, it is obvious that having a relatively smoothly operated industry should be of utmost importance. Even though the contribution made by agriculture may appear to be relatively small considering the above stated figures in relation to the country's population of 50,98 million (*Stats SA. May 2013*), the truth remains that without it a lot may diminish.

How do historical events affect the agricultural industry?

Even though this prestigious industry has been improvingly prosperous in the past era, its success was limited to specified regulations which marginalised a large proportion of other keen citizens to contribute to its prosperity. This fact could therefore imply that the ultimate potential of the industry was not realised due to the restrictions that were set back then. From this point, a further implication could be determined, and that is, in order to unlock the utmost potential of the South African agricultural sector, one of the factors that should be considered is to have an increase in the number of agricultural producers who will be assisted accordingly without any limits.

Due to the restrictions that have been introduced decades ago, it became a norm that citizens who were classified in any ethnic group other than that of

Caucasians, would only participate in farming as general farm employees. Amongst others, this is undoubtedly one of the reasons that resulted in the newer generations of the formally marginalised groups to develop a negative perception on the business of farming whereby they associated it with oppression, illiteracy, dirt, and all other demoralising factors you can think of. This obviously created the wrong impression about the farming business to majority of the oppressed population. Therefore, the consequence of this fact demands that the transformation process should also cater for changing the mind-set of the younger generation of the previously marginalised citizens.

The change that was brought upon by the new era resulted in the need to transform this industry by allowing all aspiring citizens to make their own desired contributions without any prejudice. This therefore gave birth to what could be referred to as Developing Agriculture.

2

THE CONCEPT OF DEVELOPING AGRICULTURE

What is Developing Agriculture?

First of all, Developing Agriculture can be viewed as a major component of the entire agricultural sector, which aims to transform its previously marginalised farming producers from the developing level to the point of being fully-fledged commercial farmers within a reasonable amount of time. Although the amount of time required to transform these farmers cannot be specified, it remains important to bear in mind that it should be done with as minimal delay as possible as this will assist in keeping up the momentum of its progress while avoiding any time-related setbacks.

The impact of Developing Agriculture on the industry as a whole in contrast to Commercial Agriculture

If the industry was to be divided into two main sub-sectors, i.e. the commercial and the developing divisions, the developing part will surely weigh more than the commercial part simply because it has much more elements that need to be addressed. Examples of such elements may include but not restricted to the extension services that is required by developing farmers, the amount and type of support they need in order for them to show any progress, new innovations and technology creations that are discovered by researchers, mentorship, knowledge transfer and skills development. Whereas in commercial agriculture, the main focus is on the sustainability of its achievements. Nevertheless, this does not imply that commercial farmers will not be in need of new farming innovations. They'll still need information on issues like new farming machinery, new animal breeds and new crop cultivars. It therefore makes sense to conclude that the component that causes the imbalance in the farming equation should be given more attention since it influences the well-being of the entire industry as well as that of the country's economy.

Diagram 1: Indicates the imbalance caused by Developing Agriculture in the entire the industry

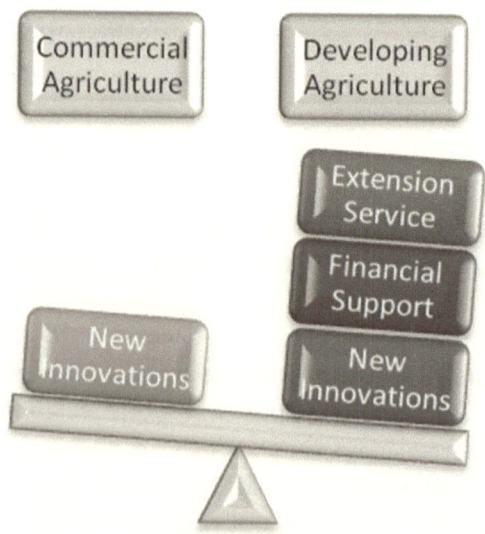

The major objective of Developing Agriculture

Even though this industry has been sufficiently nurtured and supported in the past, its transformation requires it to be equally or in some instances, even more supportive to emerging farmers in order to ensure equal positioning of all aspirant farmers in terms of their scale of farming, profitability and independence in producing their products. This indirectly depicts one of the objectives of developing agriculture which is to increase the number of commercialised farmers by uplifting new and developing farmers through the provision of all necessary requirements of the farming business. The more this objective is achieved, the more there'll be farm lands that will be fully utilised, which will entail having more agricultural products and will contribute towards having increased supplies of food and raw materials. As a consequence of this, the affordability of basic foods and the economy will directly be influenced.

With all that's been said and done thus far, the current times can be declared as "the new agricultural era".

3

TRANSFORMATION AS A FACTOR OF DEVELOPING AGRICULTURE

What does transformation entail?

In its simplest sense, Transformation is a process that seeks to convert its target from a somewhat poorer condition to a more improved and/or advanced position. So, one can immediately see that positive change is the main issue here. In this instance, developing farmers will be labelled as the target to be enriched from a position that is regarded to be more inferior (when compared to beneficiaries of the past regime) to a level of equality as far as the success of operating a farming business is concerned. Since this process is intended to make developing farmers to prosper in the business of farming, it could be regarded as a major factor that operates under the umbrella of Developing Agriculture.

Measuring transformation

The fact that the development of this industry focuses solely on previously disadvantaged groups of farmers can actually derive the standards that need to be attained by the very same developing farmers. The farming level of successfully commercialised farmers of the previous regime can be used as a yardstick that could measure the progress of developing the farmers of the current era. In other words, developing farmers should aim to reach the level of the current commercialised farmers who benefitted from the previous era, in terms of their scale of farming, profit margins, production skills and independence of their farming businesses.

Having said that, this statement may give rise to a question that asks: if this industry has proven to be prospering and succeeding prior to its new era, then why should it go through this transformation phase?

One can make a further argument by stating that transformation is a lengthy process that starts by reducing or completely halting the momentum and achievements of the industry, then why go through it?

Well the answer to both these appropriate questions can be justified in one word, which is Synergy.

The theory of Synergy

The theory of synergy denotes that the effect of combining more than one force should be greater than the impact or result of the individual ability. So, rephrasing this theory with reference to Developing Agriculture will read as follows: without setting any restrictions to all contributions made by various competent role players, the collective results of the industry will surely yield results that will be greater than the individual ability which will enrich its eventual success. This theory clearly indicates that any form of marginalisation on other potential contributors will restrict the ultimate potential of the industry, since it will only allow a certain proportion of citizens to contribute to it. Thus an increase in the number of competent farmers will ensure increased synergy levels.

How does this theory relate to Developing Agriculture?

With an increment in the number of contributing farmers (without necessarily considering their scale of farming at this stage), the South African agricultural sector will realise improved production rates of agricultural products. Should this be achieved, then the shortage and unaffordability of basic food and raw materials will surely be a problem of the past. The table and graph below illustrates the impact of this theory as achieved thus far in the potato and beef producing sub-sectors. The data suggests that both these sectors have shown considerable improvements in transforming its developing farmers.

Table 1: Demonstrating the concept and impact of synergy

	Normally	Synergy
Synergy theory	1 + 1 = 2	1 + 1 = 3
Potato production	1016 000 tonnes during 1986-87	2167 000 tonnes during 2010-11
Beef cattle produced	596 000 tonnes during 1986-87	819 000 tonnes during 2010-11

Data source: Abstract of agricultural statistics. 2012—Department of Agriculture, Forestry and Fisheries

Under normal circumstances, adding an individual's effort to another individual effort will result in a double of the same effort; this is indicated numerically as 1 + 1 = 2. However, with the achievement of synergy, when two efforts are combined, the impact of these efforts should be greater than the impact of the individual ability, which is why it's indicated as 1 + 1 = 3. So, the theory simply illustrates that a proper combination of influences will enhance the outcome of the intended objective. Now let's relate this theory to the growth of the beef and potato sub-sectors.

Graph 1: The impact of synergy in the Beef and Potato industries

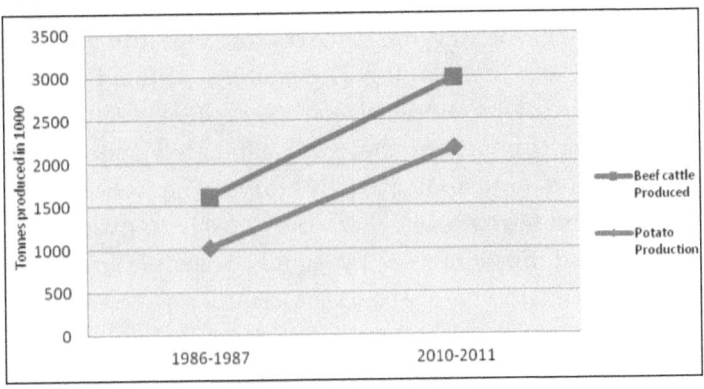

The production of both these commodities has continued to grow by significant margins from post 1994. Although the growth in production could be as a result of a combination of factors, one of the reasons will surely be the increase in the number of producers. So then, it makes reasonable sense to assume that the number of new competent farmers is dominated by previously disadvantaged farmers who benefitted from some of the farmer development programs of the current era. To make this assumption more concrete, there are quite significant numbers of previously commercialised farmers who sold their farms or discontinued their farming businesses either by choice or due to other forceful circumstances. With this note in mind, the production of both commodities has grown gradually which creates a strong belief that the number of contributing developing farmers has risen.

Subsequent to the theory indicated above, the individual competence of every contributing farmer is of utmost importance since it directly contributes towards the collective result. It is for this reason that the primary objective of developing agriculture should place much more of its emphasis on every individual farmer or farming operation that will ultimately contribute towards the industrial objective of having successfully transformed farmers who were previously disadvantaged. This should be achieved by simply transforming them from the developing phase to the clearly developed level of farming.

What should this process focus on?

It needs to be understood that this transformation process will not necessarily be starting entirely from point zero, but will be a continuation of what was initiated decades ago. The only difference is that the current system will focus primarily on the previously marginalised group. However, the process should not necessary attempt to let history repeat itself by oppressing keen and competent farmers who've already been commercialised by the past regime, but should rather do away with the limitations of the past so as to realise the maximum potential of South African agriculture. It should only aim to balance the equation by boosting those who were deliberately neglected prior to the new era of developing agriculture. The consequences of repeating what was done previously will be unbearable since they'll yield the same negative results of the past which is not maximising the potential of the industry.

Having such a situation in the current times will surely worsen the position of the industry.

Given the increased human populations, having a reduced supply of agricultural products would be extremely disastrous because increased populations require the same increase in basic foods and raw material.

What should this process refrain from?

The process of transformation should preferably transpire without negatively affecting or demoralising the current commercial farmers who benefited from the previous regime by showing any negligence or making them feel less valuable as this will cause an even bigger gap between the current position and the utmost point of success that is desired by the industry.

4

DISTINGUISHING THE DIFFERENT LEVELS OF FARMING IN DEVELOPING AGRICULTURE

Why is it necessary to make a distinction between the different levels of farming?

It is quite inevitable that the dawn of change will in most cases (if not always) start with a decline in the momentum of the current status, especially if the change deals with developing human persona or livelihoods. Although marginalised farmers of the previous era have been restricted in the same way, their individual capabilities were quite different. Some of them were much more capable than others in terms of their ability to farm with limited resources and without any support. Those who were somehow able to produce any agricultural products for income generation would settle for supplying their products locally to the informal market. Whilst on the other hand, the rest of them would only produce crops and rear farm animals only for subsistent use. Due to such reasons, it then becomes important to categorise the beneficiaries of developing agriculture according to their potential and different levels of achievement. After all, not all beneficiaries will be starting from the same level. This will automatically form the basis of determining the type and form of assistance that is required by beneficiaries of a specified category. It should be obvious enough that developing farmers who are farming at the lowest level whilst having the urge and capacity to grow will need more attention when compared to other developing farmers. Therefore, the distinction between the different levels of farming as well as the description of various types of farmers may not only be important but will also make it easier to measure the progress and growth of every farming operation that benefits from the transformation process.

The description of "Previously Disadvantaged Farmers"

Before elaborating on the descriptions and distinctions of the different levels of farming, it is imperative to derive a common understanding of what exactly does the all-encompassing term of "previously disadvantaged farmers" refer to. Without making any reference to ethnicity or benefits that existed prior to the new era of developing agriculture, previously disadvantaged farmers can basically be regarded as those who can be characterised by the following factors:

a) Those who were restricted from getting any sort of assistance and/or support
b) Those who couldn't have access to basic resources of establishing viable farming businesses
c) Those who didn't realise the business component of farming
d) As well as those who used to farm in subsistence

These are some of the aspects that contributed towards marginalising other farmers whilst their complete opposites are the reason why others were commercialised. Although it is mainly a combination of the above factors that resulted in the restrictions of the industry, it is the first two points that were the main contributors. Therefore, this implies that these are the two most important factors that should be prioritised on in Developing Agriculture.

A distinction between the different levels of farming

The main levels of farming; the types of farmers associated with them as well as their categories can be distinguished in the diagram below.

Diagram 2: Representing the different types of farmers and their levels of farming

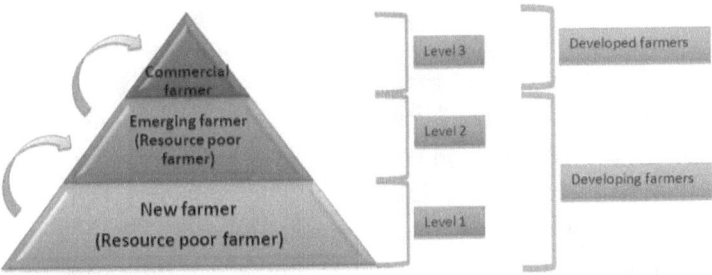

The diagram above clearly shows that there are three main levels of farming from which farmers operate their production enterprises as profit generating businesses. From these levels of farming, the first two fall under the category of developing farmers. If and where possible, some other subdivisions can be added within the main levels of farming, which will make the measurement of improved farmers much easier. Furthermore, the diagram shows the level which all farmers aim to attain, and that is the commercial farming level. Once developing farmers attain this level, they do not qualify to be regarded as developing farmers anymore and will therefore be phased out of Developing Agriculture.

However, bear in mind that the diagram only illustrates profit driven farming enterprises and not other types of farming operations like subsistent farmers.

The various types of farmer levels are described below. Different individuals may structure their descriptions differently, but will have a very similar meaning.

Subsistent farmers

This term is used to describe farmers who simply produce crops or rear farm animals for their own consumption only. Such farmers are not necessarily profit driven and don't apply any business management skills in their farming operations. They only need to have a fair amount of technical knowledge and skills to keep their production going. Usually, they do not require any of the commonly required agricultural resources since they only farm in the backyards of their living areas or on fairly small pieces of land. Therefore they are not faced with the common challenges of developing agriculture. Hence they are suitably classified under food security programs as opposed to Developing Agriculture.

New (also referred to as beginner or entrant) farmers

As the name clearly explains, this term is used to describe farmers who have most recently established their new farming businesses. Such businesses will in most cases be initiated at the lowest scale of production (but should yet be profitable) which will give the inexperienced farmer room to grow their personal competence together with that of the business.

Small scale farmers

This level of farming could be added as sub-level of new farmers since new farmers will in most cases start their businesses at a small scale. Nevertheless, not all newly established farming operations start at a small scale level; hence this depicts the major difference between these two levels. Small scale farming is one of those farming terms which are commonly spoken about but do not have a true threshold point.

Resource poor farmers

Most people tend to regard resource poor farming as an additional farming level. However, this is not entirely true since it's actually a term that can be associated with a specific level of farmers. Such farmers are simply those who have either limited or no access to essential agricultural resources. Although this occurs minimally at higher levels of farming, farming with limited resources will in most cases be associated with developing farmers.

However, the norm is that, when progressing from one level of farming to another, the availability of basic resources tends to improve. Based on this statement, it can therefore be concluded that the growth in available resources has a direct influence on the growth in the level of farming.

Emerging farmers

A further distinction of farmers involved in developing agriculture is defined as emerging farmers. This term is given to farmers who have already established their farming businesses. Although they have improved or grown from the new farmers' level, they still operate at a lower scale than desired. As a result of this, these farmers will always have room to grow and expand their farming businesses. Since all farmers involved in developing agriculture have the desire to grow and sustain their existing or newly established farming businesses, they are generally referred to as emerging farmers.

Commercial farmers (can be referred to as large scale farmers)

Emerging farmers will always have a few elements in common, but the most common one is their desire to reach the commercial farming level. Ironically, commercial farming has not yet been clearly defined in a way that is generally known and accepted. To prove this controversy, various literature sources have shown different views regarding the definition of a commercial farmer. Nevertheless, it has over the years been associated with producing for a market/for selling, the scale of production, profit margins obtained, competency and independence from any form of assistance. Crop Estimate Committee (2004) and Stats SA (2010) suggest that a commercial farmer is a person who produces agricultural products intended for the market. But *Johan Kirsten, 2011*, argues that if measured by gross farm income, small-scale farmers should be considered as any producer with a gross farm income below R500 000 a year. Both definitions show that the industry has no holistic definition and no common agreement on the factors to be emphasized on when defining this term. Nevertheless, having a true and distinctive definition is not the main concern at this point since the above factors contribute in at least differentiating commercialised farmers from the rest. The main point of concern is the thresholds of the factors that have been associated with it. Either way, it should be realised that farmers operating at this level do not fall within the parameters of Developing Agriculture any longer as they are already developed.

As confusing as this may appear, commercial farming is further subdivided into two more levels, i.e. fully fledged commercial farmers and semi-commercial farmers. Since commercial farming is not clearly defined on its own, the challenge of defining its subdivisions may be quite uneasy. So, making reasonable assumptions may be the next best thing considering the fact that these terms are quite self-explanatory.

I. Fully fledged commercial farmers

With reference to popular belief and the self-explanatory term, fully fledged commercial farmers are farmers who have reached their ultimate level of farming, meaning that they produce for specified markets, they are somewhat (if not totally) independent, they also have possession of all the required resources, quite experienced and generate substantial profits from their farming businesses. Such businesses have in most cases shown an element of sustainability as they are usually successfully managed across several generations.

II. Semi-commercial

This refers to farmers who have progressed from the emerging phase but still not quite fully fledged. Their scale of production may be impressive and may be generating lucrative profits, but could rely on some assistance in order for them to attain successfully functioned farming businesses. Furthermore, although such businesses may be succeeding, they may not have proven their sustainability over extended periods. Again, it may be difficult to make a clear distinction since there aren't any threshold values attached to these terms.

The above mentioned points create the impression that developing farmers may constantly attempt to attain a target that is not clearly defined nor clearly measured. Therefore, the implication thereof is that they could reach the commercial farming level without realising it, which simply implies that they'll always be referred to as emerging farmers. Should things continue to remain this way, then the success of Developing Agriculture will never be clearly measured and emerging farmers will forever remain emerging. So measuring the success rate of Developing Agriculture becomes compulsory.

5

INDICATORS OF MEASURING THE PROGRESS OF DEVELOPING AGRICULTURE

It should be evident by now that measuring the progress of any continuous process should be supported by predefined threshold values which will be aligned to every level of achievement. Failure to do so will lead to the difficulty of evaluating improvement. Although threshold values will surely aid in determining the distinction between the different levels of farming, there are indicators that could be used to at least gauge progress.

Start by differentiating developing farmers from developed farmers

In order to derive a formula that will enhance the progress of emerging farmers, the distinction between developing and developed farmers needs to be recognised to ensure that the appropriate support is provided to the most relevant beneficiaries. Making this a prerequisite of assessing the progress made by developing farmers is essential as there are different types of farmer levels in the industry. Since a common understanding of the threshold value and the absolute definition of commercial farming have not yet been determined, the upliftment of developing farmers remains to be one of the best indicators of evaluating the progress of Developing Agriculture.

In order for farmers to qualify for assistance under the scope of Developing Agriculture, and for them to be classified as developing, they need to have room for growth and be able to advance from a lower farming level to the next. Developed farmers do not have room for growth within the scope of Developing Agriculture as they do not fall within the two lowest levels of farming. That's why they cannot be declared as developing any longer.

Measuring the success rate of Developing Agriculture

However, the success rate of developing the industry through its transformation process should still be measured. This could perhaps be done by determining other indicators that can be used to determine its progression. Some of the indicators that could be used to determine the success rate of Developing Agriculture are identified as follows:

- The increase in the number of competent farmers who are able to successfully produce quality products that can be sold at competitive market prices whilst generating meaningful profits for themselves. This will ultimately

increase the level of synergism that will be brought upon by various farmers of this industry.
- Increased supply of agricultural products.
- Increased food security.
- Decreased food prices.
- Maximum utilisation of prime agricultural lands.

The prime indicator of success

Once commercial farming is clearly given a holistic definition that will be supported by threshold values, then the number of transformed farmers will be able to be clearly determined which will ultimately provide the basis of determining the success rate of Developing Agriculture. Though other levels of farming can be distinguished from others by distinct definitions, they also need threshold values that will aid in tracking the improvement made by every farmer. As things stand, raising the number of farmers who will be established through some of the transformation programs whilst ensuring a continuous production of various agricultural products is still the only absolute indicator of measuring the progress of developing agriculture. Therefore, the individual improvement achieved by developing farmers will directly influence the progression of the industry even though the threshold points of labelling them as commercial farmers are still not clear.

6

ESSENTIAL RESOURCES REQUIRED BY DEVELOPING FARMERS

What are resources?

In general business terms, resources are commonly referred to as man-made and natural elements, or a quality that a person or an organisation has which will enable it to complete an activity or can be exploited for economic purposes. Although the three most basic resources that are required for establishing or operating a farming business are capital, land and labour; there are more resources that are just as important or in some cases much more important than the most common ones. The type of resource that needs to be prioritised on when uplifting developing farmers will differ with each farmer/farming business based on their priority of needs. Always remember that the most limiting resource should preferably be the one that takes priority.

Resources required by developing farmers

Developing farmers will usually have one or a combination of the resources listed below as a limiting factor to their farming businesses

Table 2: The essential resources of establishing a farming business

Categories	Pre-primary Resource	Primary Resources	Secondary Resources
Resources	1. Independent decision making	1. Land	1. Farm machinery
		2. Capital/ finance	2. Infrastructure
		3. Knowledge and skills	3. Production inputs
		4. Passion/ Desire for farming	

Primary Resources

1. Land

It's a commonly known fact that any farming business needs land to be established as this forms the basis of any farming operation regardless of the enterprise. This issue is somewhat complex in a sense that it affects farmers in two different ways. Whilst some farmers have difficulties in gaining access to prime agricultural lands, others find it difficult to get ownership of leased lands. The latter includes lands that could either be communal, tribal owned, privately leased or from the state. The major constraint associated with such lands is that farmers become restricted to erect any permanent structures which may serve as one of the restricting factors of growing their farming businesses.

The other importance of this resource lies in the production potential of the land. This should be seriously considered when purchasing, leasing or acquiring land in any of the specified forms, since it has the power to inhibit successful agricultural production. Therefore farmers are compelled not to attempt utilising lands with minimum production abilities as it may be too expensive to invest money on such farms due to their tendency of low economic returns if obtained at all.

2. Capital/finance

Any business venture requires funding to start or continue its operation and farming is no exception to this fact. It needs to be clearly understood that farmers who are in need of capital are those who are usually at the beginning stages of their businesses. Remember that capital is money that is required to start a business. In most cases, farmers who would be in need of operational funding could have been beneficiaries of capital support or may have been assisted with any of the other primary resources at some point. The support and assistance that is being referred to, is one that will be sufficient for beneficiaries to at least commence their businesses. Those who are already in operation and in need of additional financial support (if they weren't assisted in starting these businesses) will rather be eligible for operational funding instead of capital. The significance of recognising finance as a primary resource lies in the fact that when it is accessed in sufficient amounts it creates the ability of being able to acquire any of the other resources.

3. Knowledge and skills

Technical and business competencies are some of the key requirements of farmers. Both these competencies are usually acquired through training, exposure and experience. Although it wouldn't hurt to train or expose farmers to as much knowledge and skills as possible, it is advisable to bring them into terms of understanding the advantages of specialising in commodities that are related to their enterprises, other than attempting to be "a jack of all trades". The lack of specialization will create a situation where they'll (farmers) know bits and pieces of every commodity/enterprise instead of developing thorough expertise in enterprises they are involved in.

Professionals of this industry tend to incorrectly assume and conclude that developing farmers will always have a lack of the technical know-how of farming. Considering the fact that some developing farmers of today are those who were employed as labourers over many years on commercial farms, technical knowledge and skills may be the last thing they would need. In such instances, it's the competence in agricultural business management that remains the most neglected but yet important competency that is required by such developing farmers.

4. Farming passion

Without a self-driven passion, no one will succeed in any business and farming is one of them. Unfortunately this is one of those resources which cannot be provided to farmers by anyone, but must come from within the farmer. So this makes it the most unique and essential resource that farmers must have. Most people tend to confuse farmers who possess a passion for farming, with those who have a strong desire of generating income through farming. The latter may not necessarily be a passionate farmer because his/her main concern is the financial benefit associated with it. The difference here is that the passionate farmer will manage the enterprise as a business by engaging the right agricultural practices throughout the entire production season which will ultimately maximise his economic returns, as opposed to the one who would settle for any amount of money that comes their way. This refers to farmers who would for instance plant crops without applying fertilizer or those who rear livestock without providing proper feeds. In both instances, these farmers could generate something even if it will not be the maximum and the production season will be prolonged.

However, the most worrying concern about the farming passion is that people tend to develop it at an elderly age. It is therefore a minimum percentage of young individuals who have the desire of taking farming as their primary career. As time progresses, there seem to be an increase in the number of young and keen candidates in the industry (depending on the area). On the other hand, now that there's a considerable amount of youngsters who are beginning to show a keen interest in this industry, they tend to follow the agricultural profession route as opposed to becoming the actual farmers. This implies that the challenge of engaging young blood in the farming industry still remains although its focus has shifted from not having young candidates at all to having them more as agricultural professionals other than farmers.

Secondary Resources

1. Farm machinery

This refers to all the machinery required to operate any farming business depending on its type of enterprise. These resources are those that allow farmers to either produce their commodity or permit them to farm with ease, namely tractors, implements and combine harvesters to mention a few. They are regarded as secondary resources because farmers do not necessarily have to own them since they can always outsource them from other farmers who offer such services as contractors.

2. Infrastructure

Although high tech infrastructure may be ideal for farming at profitable levels, most developing farmers tend to be innovative in erecting their own basic structures such as piggery units, poultry houses, animal kraals, nursery structures and storage facilities. As important as it is, it's in most cases least likely to prevent beginner farmers from starting their own farming businesses. Hence, it's categorised as a secondary resource. Although some high tech infrastructures may be viewed as luxury items, they actually serve important purposes that are meaningful to the farming business. Examples of these include heated tunnels which will ensure all year round production of crops, and automated poultry houses which ensure that the right amount of feed is fed to the chickens at the right time whilst minimising the amount of manual labour required to operate the unit.

3. Production inputs

Production inputs are always a prerequisite in every farming enterprise. When sufficient funds are available, this will not be redeemed as a limiting factor of production since funds can cater for all production inputs. As a matter of fact, there are still substantial numbers of farmers who rely on publicly or privately funded projects and donations as their main source of inputs, without which, all farming activities could completely stop with immediate effect.

The importance of categorising the farmer resources

It is important for the above stated resources to be divided into primary and secondary categories. Grouping them in this way will assist in determining those that cannot be compromised in order to create any slight chance of establishing or operating a farming business. Obviously it's the primary resources that form the basis of developing successful farming business. The secondary resources on the other hand are still quite important, depending on the farmer's situation. There is pretty much a significant amount of developing farmers who still view these secondary resources as factors that hinder their farming success. However, these secondary resources can always be accommodated by the capital/finance if it's acquired in sufficient amounts as a primary resource.

Timing is of the essence when providing or acquiring essential resources of the farming business

In cases where farmers get their resources as beneficiaries of any projects or funding programs from various agricultural institutions, care should be taken to ensure that all resources are made available to them in the right form and supplied at the right time. Timing has always been of the most significant essence when supporting developing farmers. For instance, providing farmers with seed and fertilizer too late in the planting season spells disaster instead of farmer support.

The additional and key category of essential resources

Most people who are involved in the development of this industry have a tendency of incorrectly assuming that with all the primary and secondary resources in order, farmers will reach their success of being fully developed commercial farmers.

In addition to the two categories stated above, there is a category that may be more essential. The resource that falls within this category is purely intrapersonal, meaning that it solely depends on the human qualities and commitment levels that are possessed by the individual farmer.

Pre-Primary Resource

I. Independent decision making

As a commonly known assumption of this industry, professional agriculturalists and various institutions are of the impression that the possession of the above stated resources will ensure the success of developing farmers. As a result of this, much time is dedicated to the provision of such resources to farmers, and more, farmers are always encouraged to acquire them. Yet there is still a significant amount of developing farmers who do not improve on their farming enterprises but instead worsen their farming levels in spite of being provided with all the required primary and/or secondary resources. This fact proves beyond any doubt that there's a need and importance of being able to consolidate and manage resources well. Therefore the ability to independently make sound decisions that will best benefit the business is vital. The independence of the decision making process needs to be emphasized since it creates room for farmers to be able to develop their own future competence. This simply implies that farmers will also grow mentally instead of just growing their businesses. It is always important to understand that the growth of any business venture should go hand in hand with the growth of its management ability.

Given the fact that the pre-primary resource is a human quality, it can be concluded that the success of each farmer begins within oneself.

Remember: Farmers may not always know the most vital resource required by them

Agricultural professionals or mentors need to understand that developing farmers may not necessarily know the most vital resource they need, especially when it's a human quality trait. That's why it's important for farmers to determine their most limiting factors together with other experienced persons.

7

METHODS OF ACQUIRING ESSENTIAL NEEDS IN A FARMING BUSINESS

The upliftment of developing farmers can be measured by the farmers improved scale of production which is highly reliant on the availability of the essential needs of production. There are quite significant numbers of farmers in the South African farming industry whose growth and success is restricted by the unavailability of essential resources. This issue is prevalent particularly with grain crop producers since they need quite a considerable amount of financial power to start and sustain their businesses. Bear in mind that these are commodities that need to be grown at fairly large scales in order for them to be viable. The reason why some of them remain dependent is due to facts that they are forced to use loans to purchase production inputs like seed, fertilizer, chemicals and diesel; whilst hiring some of the essential machinery from the very same loan. Frequently hired machinery includes tractors, planters, combine harvesters, fertilizer spreaders and boom sprayers. It is primarily due to such reasons that they then spend a lot of their income and profits on repaying loans and paying for the hired machinery and services which leaves them with no option but to go through the same process continuously without gaining the financial independence. The moral of this story clearly shows that having access to some of the essential resources of farming is of utmost importance since it can be a stimulator of growth.

The above facts provides reasons for creating a process that will assist in determining and acquiring the most essential resources that can be used to the benefit of the farming business. The derived process can be used to determine various factors which include:

I. Measuring the developing farmer's current position (in terms of resources available)
II. Determining the farmers' most important needs
III. Deriving the appropriate process that should be followed in attaining resources
IV. Indication of the farmers' achievements.

The importance of this cycle

This process is in the form of a cycle which is also a simplified guide that should be followed by farmers when attempting to acquire essential resources. Obtaining important resources can be viewed as an indication of improvement amongst developing farmers since it allows farmers to spend less on hiring essential machinery and/or services and it also makes farmers to operate their businesses more efficiently and independently.

> Remember: The factors stated above are some of those that are associated with commercial farming.

The Acquisition of needs cycle

Even though the activities of this process will be implemented by the farmer, they should preferably be steered by an agriculturalist that has the relevant expertise. Such persons will not only help the farmer to determine his/her needs, but they will also advise them on where to go as well as the prerequisites required. The benefiting farmer should preferably be involved in the determination and implementation of all these activities as it will indirectly unlock the independent decision making ability in them, which forms the basis of an exit strategy.

Diagram 3: The Acquisition of Needs Cycle (TANC)

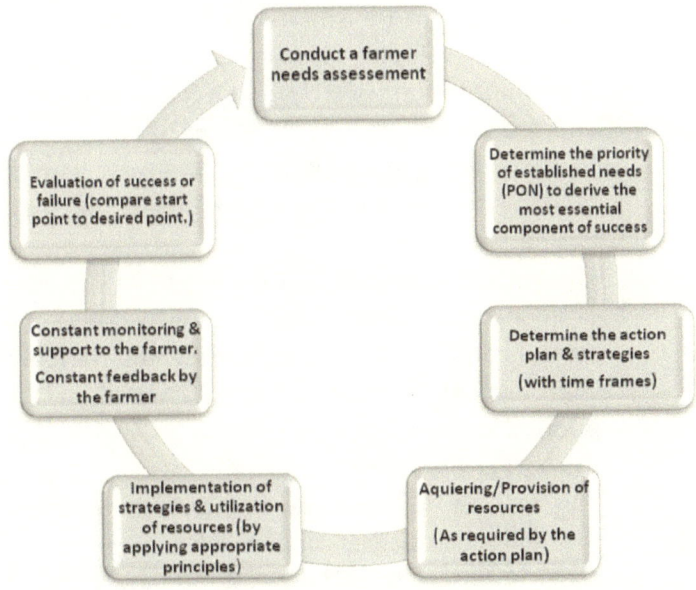

> Note: It is not advisable for farmers to see themselves through this process even though it's possible. Going through it with another individual will not only assist in determining other important contributing factors which may not be known to the farmer, but the farmer will also have a supervisory mentor who will guide them through it.

This process clearly illustrates the activities that need to be followed when determining the farmer's progress rate through the acquisition of resources.

1. The first activity of the process involves the determination of the farmer's needs. This will assist in establishing the requirements that are needed to ensure the farmer's progress. The needs of developing farmers may and/or will vary with different farmers based on their commodity and area amongst others. Hence it's important to conduct this activity with every farmer (particularly at the beginning stages of their business).

2. Thereafter, these needs should be put in order of importance, which will be used to derive the most limiting factor that hinders the farmer's improvement. Therefore the attainment of the prioritized need/s will be used as an indicator of the farmer's progress.

3. This will be followed by the determination of the action strategies that will be employed in order to ensure the attainment of the prescribed needs. It's always important to determine this

prior to determining the types of resources to be provided or acquired, since it will assist in determining the most important resources that will be required to put the action plan in operation.

4. The provision or acquiring of resources can then follow. It needs to be strongly emphasized that some resources may need to come solely from the farmer, whilst some of them may need to be provided to them as part of the assistance that comes from some of the transformation programs. These resources should be seen as tools that will guarantee that the strategies derived in the action plan are realised.

5. Implementation of strategies and the utilization of acquired resources will entail making use of the resources in order to achieve the strategized actions.

6. In order to ensure that farmers are progressing in the right direction, they should give their mentors/extension officers regular feedback and should in turn get constant monitoring and support from their mentees/farmers. This step will aid in determining whether the applied actions and activities are in line with the predefined needs. If not so, then they can be rectified before any significant damage arises.

Typically, the norm of the industry is that monitoring and support is usually provided to farmers through mentorship from commercial farmers who are within close proximity to them, highly experienced in the particular commodity they are assisting in and still active in their own farming businesses. Although this makes up good criteria for selecting mentors, the only threat with such an approach is that it creates an element of contradiction to mentors since they are in a way expected to assist other farmers to compete with them.

7. Thereafter, the final evaluation will follow. This should be done by determining whether the predetermined objective/s has been attained or not. If attained, the next prioritised need should be tackled. If not, then the most appropriate corrective action must be taken which could be repeated until the need is eventually attained.

Nevertheless it needs to be clearly understood that, the successful completion of one cycle may not necessarily indicate the movement from one level of farming to the next, but could clearly show that the farmer has improved by attaining his/her prioritized need. Furthermore, it may be important to realise that prioritized needs of each farmer or farming operation may not remain constant but may vary from time to time. In addition to time, these priorities will also differ with the level of farming, the produced commodity and geographical positioning.

Some of the prioritised farmer needs can be achieved simultaneously in the same cycle of TANC; for example, a farmer can make efforts to acquire additional funding for expanding into another farming enterprise whilst finding a market for the very same enterprise. Whereas some of them will need to be tackled one at a time since they could be prerequisites to other needs. For instance, when the developing farmer's need is to acquire knowledge and skills of a particular commodity through training, they will surely need to undergo the training before attempting to start with the enterprise.

Even though all of the steps and activities are important, one of them is very crucial in a sense that it's the first step that shapes the route of the farmer's progress. That's activity number two in the process, which entails putting the identified famer needs in order of importance.

Is it really necessary to determine the "Priority of Needs" (PON) of a farming operation?

The importance of this activity is often realised with farmers who tend to show significant improvements in a particular aspect of their farming businesses whilst lacking on another aspect. This results in having two opposite extremes which affects the overall progress of the business. A good example of such an instance is a farmer who increases his/her production of a particular commodity without formally securing a market in advance by signing a forward contract. Although the farmer may have successfully produced the commodity at a larger scale, the success of increasing his/her quantity of products appears to be quite worthless since the excess products will not be able to be sold simply because the market gap that existed at the beginning of the production season is no longer there. Thus the farmer incurs more costs as opposed to increased profitability. In this instance the farmer was supposed to prioritise on formally securing the market before prioritising on the actual production. Therefore his/her efforts appear to be a big failure other than an improvement.

How do we determine the need/s to be prioritised on?

The farmer's PON can best be determined by the broken barrel method which affirms Liebig's Law of the Minimum. The law states that growth is controlled not by the total amount of resources available, but by the scarcest resource (limiting factor) [Wikipedia, 2013]. Consequently, the most limiting factor becomes the prioritised need of the farmer. In this case, the attainment of the most limiting component will automatically make the next limiting one the most prioritised one.

Diagram 4: The broken barrel method indicating the farmer's most limiting factor of success

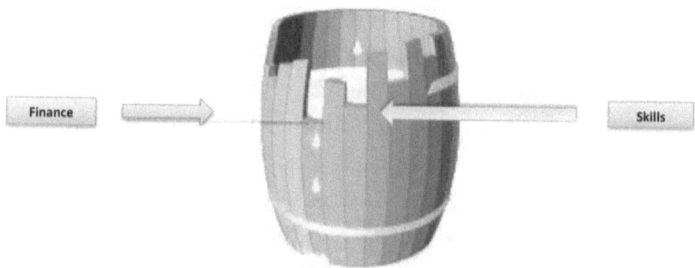

The most minimised component of the barrel will determine the most optimum factor of the water retention capacity, meaning that the water will only fill the barrel until the most restricting factor. Subsequent to this fact, it is the most limiting factor of success that will automatically become the most important factor to be prioritised on in order to improve the production and profitability of the concerned farming business. Diagram 4 gives an example of a farmer in need of finance as his/her priority. Let's assume that this is a poultry farmer who's in possession of all the infrastructure and capital items (e.g. broiler house, feeders, drinkers, gas heaters etc.) without having the financial power to buy the production inputs like chicks, feed and medication. As soon as he/she attains the necessary finance, then the next need will be tackled. If the technical knowledge and skills of operating the broiler enterprise appears to be the next limiting factor, then training should be the farmer's next need of priority.

It should now be quite clear that every developing farmer will have a broken barrel that reflects their farming position. Therefore this method can be used to illustrate the farmer's level of improvement. If the industry cannot derive threshold values of developed farmers, then it can surely develop the lowest acceptable level of the water in the broken barrel method. This means that if defined, the very same barrel system can be used to determine the most basic resources required to initiate a farming business. Furthermore, this method can also be used to classify the different levels of farming in which each a farmer operates in. The only thing that needs to be done will be to draw lines (around the barrel) at different heights of the barrel which will represent the different levels of farming.

Diagram 5: A barrel illustrating the various levels of farming according to the farmer's achievement

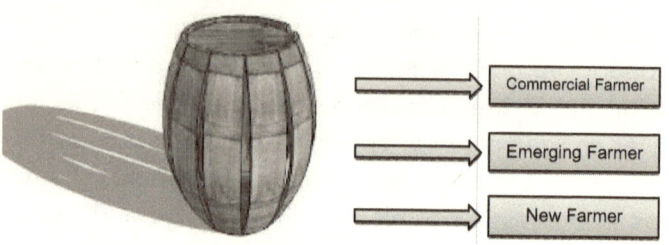

Since it's now understood that once the limiting factor is achieved, the broken piece that represents it will be rectified which means that the water retention capacity of the barrel will improve and will subsequently indicate the farmer's success. However, the farmer's achievement of a particular need does not guarantee that the broken link will be filled to the top. It will only ensure an increase in the water holding capacity of the barrel (which equates to improvement), but may only be up to a particular level and not necessarily to the top. The following scenario illustrates an example to this theory:

If a vegetable farmer has a vision and capacity to expand into a broiler production enterprise that will produce 1500 birds per cycle and requires a start-up capital of R150 000 but only manages to acquire R100 000, this farmer will have to settle for producing 1000 birds per cycle. Although this shows that the farmer has improved his farming business by successfully introducing another enterprise, he still didn't do it according to his vision and capacity. In this instance the broken piece will be filled by two thirds which is definitely not to the top. As a result of that, this will clearly indicate the successful progress made by this developing farmer and the industry, but does not necessarily imply that the particular need has been fulfilled to capacity. On the other hand, if the farmer's vision was to be fulfilled according to his vision, it would still not be a clear illustration of him being declared as a commercial farmer.

Even though this method strengthens the evidence of the farmer's success, it still requires threshold values for it to clearly indicate the point at which a farmer will be declared commercial. It therefore proves beyond reasonable doubt that the need to derive threshold values is eminent in this industry regardless of the type of method used to determine a farmer's growth.

8

CHALLENGES THAT ARISE WITH TRANSFORMING THE INDUSTRY

In order to identify the possible solutions that are required to resolve any challenging obstacle, the contributing challenges of the particular matter need to be determined. As far as the identification of the challenges that are associated with Developing Agriculture are concerned; various individuals and institutions will have a lot of common connections. In order for the overall challenges of the sector to be resolved, the difficulties that are experienced solely by farmers cannot constitute the scope of problems that will lead the industry towards its success if and when resolved. It is the challenges that are experienced across the entire scope of Developing Agriculture that needs to be identified and corrected. People are often mistaken by assuming that it is only the farmers who are faced with challenges that delay the progress of the industry. This assumption comes as a result of the fact that farmers' success is used as the main indicator of the progress made by the transformation process of the industry.

The first common mistake made by farmers when attempting to access support

Though individual farmers need various forms of assistance in order for them to be transformed into fully fledged commercial farmers, they have often shown signs of trying to access assistance from institutions that do not specialise in the type of service that they require. This qualifies as a challenge on its own, because it shows that some developing farmers cannot differentiate the different roles played by various institutions.

Understanding the roles played by different stake holders of the agricultural industry

Due to the above stated reason, it becomes important to understand that the roles played by the servants of the industry will have a direct and sometimes an indirect influence on farmers' success. Therefore it is vital to identify the challenges that are faced by every contributing role player of the industry. But, this process will start with the identification of various role players and the roles they each play.

Table 3: Identifying the major role players together with their respective roles

Type of role player	Description	Major role/s in the industry
Individual developing farmer	Farmers who are still at the developing level. Such farmers will usually prioritize on their individual well-being other than the ultimate progress of the industry even though it will have a direct impact on the industry.	The production and supply of agricultural products while generating profits to survive and sustain their livelihoods and farming businesses
Co-operative farmers	Farmers who attain their farming goal collectively other than individually	The same role as the individual farmer, but farmers operating in a co-operative will achieve in partnership with their co-operative members
Individual agriculturalists	Professional/skilled agriculturalists who are either self-employed or employed by agricultural institutions	Serves farmers with relevant farmer support services. Usually employed by agricultural institutions
Agricultural institutions involved in developing agriculture	Various institutions making varied contributions to the industry	Assist farmers according to their area of specialization to ensure that they progress from one level of farming to the other

Private consultants	Individually established companies that seek to speed up the process of uplifting developing farmers	Assist in Uplifting developing farmers by applying their personal expertise

Challenges associated with each role player

Now that the major role players of developing agriculture have been identified, let's look at the challenges that are associated with each role player. This table will only illustrate the challenges that affect the improvement of developing farmers as opposed to the generalised challenges that are experienced and associated with every role player of the industry.

Table 4: The main challenges faced by each role player who contributes to Developing Agriculture

		Individual developing farmer	Developing Co-operative farmers	Individual agriculturalists	Agricultural institutions involved in developing agriculture
Commonly Identified Challenges		Access to suitable agricultural land	Access to suitable agricultural land	Blurred understanding of developing farmers	Blurred understanding of developing farmers
		Access to appropriate financing	Access to appropriate financing	Minimum or no relevant experience	Reluctance to form collaborations with relevant stakeholders
		Adequate Infrastructure	Adequate Infrastructure	No or limited collaboration with other experts	Attempting to attain success in solo
		Compatibility in agricultural business management	Compatibility in agricultural business management	Occupying positions that are not related to their area of specialisation	Tendency to be more profit driven as opposed to providing assistance to developing farmers
		Technical competence (knowledge and skills)	Technical competence (knowledge and skills)	Reluctance to improve knowledge base	Lack of sustainability in established farmer support programs
		Market access	Market success		
		Sustainability of their farming achievements	Sustainability of their farming achievements		
			Group dynamics		

Individual Developing Farmer

1. Access to suitable agricultural land

The issue of getting access to the most suitable land for farming purposes has become a problem to an extent that farmers accept any piece of land that is offered to them. It is due to this reason that farmers do not take time to assess the land for its farming potential. Since it's not every piece of land that is best suitable for agricultural purposes, farmers need to take time to assess lands that are made available to them for farming purposes. Farms should be assessed by considering the size of the land in relation to the desired enterprise, the farms' soil potential, climatical conditions of the region where the farm is located, available and non-available resources as well as any competition of the commodity/ies that are most suitable to be produced on the farm. Gaining access to land that has all the basic resources of farming (which could be natural or man-made) will surely reduce some of the risks that are associated with agricultural production, and will ultimately reduce the risks that are apparent to the business of farming. Should farmers accept lands that are not ideal for farming purposes, then they may be exposed to some of the following risk factors:

- The production of crops on soils with marginal potential may yield poor results
- Growing crops on dryland (where there's no access to irrigation water) will increase the risk of being affected by drought

- Raising broilers in extreme cold conditions with poor heating systems will always cause higher mortalities
- Rearing pigs in poorly erected structures and unfavourable conditions will yield poor quality pigs that usually take long to reach the desired maturity
- Livestock should preferably be kept on farms that have sufficient good quality pastures otherwise additional costs of leasing grazing lands or buying-in feed will be incurred

In addition to all of the above, there's another land related difficulty that poses a serious threat to the industry. Although it's actually meant to be of assistance to developing farmers, the redistribution of farm lands (through the land reform programs) to keen applicants doesn't always serve the actual intended purpose. Through these programs, farmers are in most cases given farms (on lease agreements) that do not suit their farming abilities. In other words, they are allocated with farms that are either too big for the type of enterprises they want to pursue, or they don't have sufficient funds to utilise at least half of the farm. Therefore this results in the industry to have reduced supplies of agricultural products considering the fact that the industry loses the amount of products that were produced on these farms prior to them being bought and handed over to new beneficiaries.

2.   Access to appropriate financing

Farmers operating within the parameters of Developing Agriculture in South Africa don't necessarily have a problem of finding financial institutions that are willing to fund them. The major obstacle with this point is getting access to these funds. The most frustrating thing about accessing financial support from financial institutions that are meant to assist developing farmers is the criteria used to assess whether they qualify for the funding or not. Although it is clearly understood that some of these institutions are there simply for business purposes and therefore prioritise on maximising their business profits, it appears as if they do not understand the types of farmers they are meant to serve. Some of the requirements that are made prerequisites of accessing funds are the very same things that developing farmers need to be assisted with. An example of this is collateral, where farmers are expected to have an asset that would equate or exceed the intended loan amount. In some instances, farmers are expected to submit documents like tax clearance certificates or bank statements, forgetting that some of these farmers still trade informally or they use their income directly from sales to buy inputs without even making bank deposits. This implies that having an active bank account would only be an unnecessary luxury to such farmers. In addition to this, developing farmers with a true passion for farming tend to prioritize on re-investing their profits on production inputs that will again generate meaningful profits for them, other than paying accountants certain amounts of money for audits and tax certificates. Therefore agricultural funding institutions should rather add the attainment of missing documents to be a part of the support that is provided to farmers, whilst revisiting their criteria to ensure the attainment of an ultimate win-win situation. A win-win situation is one that will not oppress any of the parties. This simply means that farmers should be able to access funds, whilst institutions make their profits.

3. Adequate Infrastructure

Although developing farmers have always been innovative regarding the infrastructure required to produce and/or store their agricultural products and inputs, the lack of proper infrastructural facilities has always proven to be a limiting factor of stabilising their farming businesses. Depending on the type of commodity under production, having a lack of infrastructure doesn't really cease the production of any product; it only poses a threat of limiting the profit margins obtained from a particular enterprise. For instance, if broilers or pigs are reared in a self-made low cost facility, they may still be reared at least to a point of generating profits although the profit margins may not be optimum. Inadequately built structures have in most cases shown signs of imbalanced lighting, poor heat retention, roof leaks and sometimes side leaks, just to mention a few. Therefore these facts suggest that having self-erected structures does not inhibit production totally, but will only negatively affect the ultimate profitability. Based on this statement, it can be concluded that it's not a lack of infrastructure that's the main problem here, but the lack of having access to appropriate infrastructure.

4.   Compatibility in agricultural business management

There are quite a lot of farmers who have proven to be technically competent in producing agricultural products over several years. Despite having this competence, these farmers are still farming at the developing farmer's level without any growth in their businesses. This is simply due to the fact that they lack the business management trait in their farming businesses. It is for this reason, that this challenge has been identified as one of the factors that inhibit farmer growth as well as that of the industry.

Most people have over the years gathered the impression that technical competence is the only or the foremost important factor of becoming a successful farmer. However, this perception is not entirely true. It is mainly due to this reason that the business management aspect of farming was neglected, hence the failure in enhancing developing farmers. It's mainly the lack in business management component that makes developing farmers who are technically competent to fail in growing their businesses. Therefore it becomes imperative to instil this as a skill to developing farmers.

5.   Technical competence (knowledge and skills)

This is one challenge that has surely been given much attention in this industry. The provision of technical skills and knowledge to developing farmers has been given so much attention to an extent that all the other requirements of having sustainable farming businesses have been somewhat neglected. On the other hand, the major difficulties of this challenge are that, (a) some farmers cannot access this information in methods that would cater for their literacy levels, (b) some of them are based in remote areas where they cannot access agricultural publications and (c) some of them do not have access to advanced technological apparatus (like computers or smart phones) that can help to access such information. Therefore it's the accessing of this information that appears to be a problem and not the availability of it.

As far as skills are concerned, they are greatly required by farmers. Just like information, technical skills have to be frequently updated and practised, particularly with technology that's getting more and more advanced. The provision of skills should be done in the most appropriate form which will suite the farmer since this will enhance the maximum uptake of skills. Therefore continuous skills development should be getting as much attention as knowledge transfer.

6. Market access

It's a known fact to all business owners that subsequent to producing a product, the product needs to be traded to the relevant market for income generation. Therefore failure to sell all products could lead to lowered or no profits. However, finding the right market to supply with the produced products is not the actual problem; the problem lies in meeting the prerequisites of supplying the formal market. For instance, certain markets will only buy products if only they meet specified requirements such as being a certain distance away from them, the size or weight specifications, specific times of supply etc. These requirements are mostly far away from the developing farmers reach. Farmers find it difficult to attain such specifications due to their limited resources. This clearly gives an indication that the access of supplying the formal market remains the biggest challenge that is faced by developing farmers. Although formal markets are not encouraged to compromise on their quality standards, they should only consider that some of their specifications do not favour developing farmers. It is however, not all formal markets that create this market barrier for developing farmers, since there are quite a number of retailers who've shown a keen interest in supporting developing farmers. Due to the above stated facts, developing farmers are forced to continuously supply the informal market even though their products are not necessarily of poor quality. However, this doesn't imply that supplying the formal market is always the best marketing chain for farmers, since trading informally can at times be advantageous especially when it comes to getting higher product prices without many specifications. The major stumbling block associated with the informal market is the quantities they purchase and the unpredictability of buyers. Thus having both markets may be the best solution for farmers although it's really the formalised market that has the restrictions.

7. Sustainability of their farming achievements

Once the growth and development of the farming business is achieved (to the level that is above the current one), the next big challenge is to ensure that it does not depreciate its value, profit margins and level of farming. So the ability to sustain the business at its newly improved level is extremely important as it forms the basis of measuring improvement. If sustainability is not achieved, the overall goal of uplifting farmers from one level to the other will not be realised. The ability of sustaining a business is directly dependent on the turnover time of its assistance amongst other things. If any assistance that is meant for farmers is provided speedily, it will allow farming operations to build their momentum which is important in ensuring the sustainability of their enterprises.

Developing Co-Operative Farmers

The descriptions of points 1 to 7 under the individual developing farmer are exactly the same and also applicable to developing co-operative farmers. Therefore, it is only group dynamics issue that will be elaborated.

8.   Group dynamics

It's probably more of a proven fact by now rather than a cliché, that farming in co-operatives or groups creates less favourable chances of succeeding in the business of farming. Although the concept of farming in co-operatives seems to be quite advantageous in principle when compared to individual farming, the actual outcome of it is vice versa. Individual farmers have been frequently advised and encouraged to form co-operatives. This was introduced as a way of stimulating knowledge and idea sharing, co-operation amongst farmers and buying inputs in bulk at lower prices. In order to promote the issue of farming in co-operatives, some farmer development programs have been specifically structured to support and assist co-operatives only. In most cases, this issue is strongly emphasised by government institutions. This raises a question that why is farming in cooperatives promoted if it has proven to yield negative results? Perhaps this creates an impression that such institutions are more focused on the number of beneficiaries they will be reporting on at the end of each financial year as opposed to concentrating on the quality of support and the sustainability of the supported farming operation. Since developing farmers are in dire need of support (particularly from the government institutions or government funded projects), they somehow become compelled to form co-operatives despite the challenges that come with them. In most cases, the challenges that are associated with farming in groups are brought upon by different views in the preferred farming practices, the difference in future plans and desires, the hunger to succeed as an individual farmer, different levels of experience, a variation in belief and varied commitment levels. However, forming an agricultural co-operative with people who are of different age groups has in many instances proven that age difference is one of the primary challenges of group dynamics. As a matter of fact, it's known to many of us that people of different age groups will have more varying views and preferences than those who are in a similar age group.

This challenge simply confirms the common belief that bringing more than one human personality together is a continuous battle, especially if these people come from different backgrounds.

Individual Agriculturalists

1. Blurred understanding of developing farmers

Agriculturalists tend to have varying views on the constituents of developing farmers. Although they are all involved in the same industry and try to attain the goal of improving developing farmers, there seems to be a problem of deriving a common understanding of what is a developing farmer in its simplest sense. That's why farmers are rendered with ineffective services that fail to see them improving. As soon as there are common grounds established with regards to the types of farmers the industry is serving, the basis of the best and the most suitable support structures will easily be formed.

2. Minimum or no relevant experience

Some agriculturalists that are meant to assist developing farmers do not have the relevant and necessary experience and skill. If the farmers' source of support is poor in knowledge, skills and experience on the dynamics of the industry, then it might be difficult to provide farmers with the relevant assistance. So then, it becomes essential for individual agriculturalists to acquire the relevant experience before trying to assist developing farmers.

3. No or limited collaboration with other specialists

Whilst collaborations between institutions have existed on several farmer development projects, individual specialists tend to make little efforts in trying to establish working relations amongst themselves. In most cases, formal relationships amongst individual specialists are made compulsory by activities or mandates of institutions that they are employed by. This clearly shows that agricultural specialists share their expertise primarily due to relations that are enforced by their job descriptions or collaboration programs between their institutions, and not necessarily by choice. If such relations were regarded to be meaningful and serious by individual specialists, then formal memberships of associations and societies like the South African Society for Agricultural Extension would be mandatory. However, these individual relationships need not be formalised at all times, informal gatherings of idea sharing should be continuous and compulsory to the individuals who are serving the industry.

4. Occupying positions that are not related to their area of specialisation

Due to reasons that are mainly related to nepotism, gender and race; there are employment positions within agricultural institutions that are being occupied by people who aren't really the most appropriate candidates. This is practiced in both the public and the private sectors of the industry. The major difference between the two sectors is the way in which they apply the reasons to fill these positions. For instance, public institutions may use political, race and gender reasons; whilst the private sector may still use the same reasons but may apply them in exactly the opposite way as compared to the public sector. Although, its institutions who deliberately impose this challenge on the industry, it is up to the individual to accept positions that are relevant to them. Failure to do so means a contribution in the shortfalls of the industry.

5. Reluctance to improve knowledge base

Since knowledge and skills continuously change, the servants of the industry need to equally improve their competence. In most cases, the older the person is the more experience they tend to have. This means that they could have been involved in the industry over many years, which poses the threat of trying to apply the same principles and practices over many years. In addition to this, it is common knowledge that elderly people tend to be reluctant to adopt new innovations. Therefore one can conclude that having knowledge and skills that have been acquired over many years doesn't necessarily entail good experience. Experience can be regarded as gaining exposure and adapting to different dynamics of the industry through different periods.

However, as far as the younger generation of individuals is concerned, they tend to adhere to what is required from them by their job descriptions as specified by their employees. Meaning that they rarely try to acquire more knowledge and skills independently other than what they are employed for.

Agricultural Institutions Involved In Developing Agriculture

1.   Blurred understanding of developing farmers

It's one thing when an individual gets an unclear understanding of a term like developing farmers, but a complete different story if it's an entire institution that displays the same uncertainty. As far as the perception of developing farmers is concerned, some institutions seem to be continuously swimming in a pool of darkness, without even noticing it. It is their failure in trying to uplift these farmers that clearly reveals that they still have a blurry understanding of developing farmers. As a result of this recurring error, there are various farmer development programs and projects that do not succeed in enriching developing farmers. In addition to this, members of the public need to understand that the major difference in the misconception of developing farmers between the individual agriculturalist and agricultural institutions is that institutions incur a lot of costs in the process of this wrong doing. However, some people are opinionated that it's mainly the leadership of such institutions that steer these programs and projects in the wrong direction. This puts the employees of such agricultural institutions in the forefront of the failure, which sometimes creates the incorrect perception that individual agriculturalists are incompetent when it's actually the institution that's been led in the wrong direction.

2. Reluctance to form collaborations with relevant stakeholders

To those who've seen several collaborations between agricultural institutions in this new era of developing agriculture, it may seem absurd for this point to be regarded as a challenge. The statement above already indicates that it's not as if there aren't any existing collaborations what so ever, it's just that these collaborated schemes do not encompass all the relevant stakeholders that can contribute in developing a farmer. As a result of this, some institutions have resorted in trying to do activities that are beyond their expertise and scope of work. It is for this reason that farmers are continuously provided with irrelevant assistance in a snow balling effect and farmer development schemes continue to fail.

3. Attempting to attain success in solo

Another identified challenge that is faced with agricultural institutions is their efforts of trying to provide farmers with most if not all the requirements they need. This is usually associated with private institutions (that are usually profit driven) that give themselves this task due to the fact that collaborations with other institutions don't always yield good results and leads to reduced profits. So then it creates an impression that the efforts they contribute in various programs of farmer transformation are not always properly invested. That's why they resort to being a "jack of all trades".

4. Tendency to be more profit driven as opposed to providing assistance to developing farmers

Many of these profit driven businesses never really possess the complete scope of resources (e.g. farm lands, funding, knowledge and skills, infrastructure or even machinery) that will ensure farmers' progress. This automatically illustrates that a single institution will not have the capacity to assist farmers with everything. Even though people are meant to believe that many agricultural institutions try their level best to assist emerging farmers, the actual interest of some of them could be the financial benefit that comes with being involved in Developing Agriculture. A very good example of these businesses are those that give farmers loans and credit on production inputs at high interest rates to an extent that farmers will not have sufficient credit reserved for them to farm independently in the next season. This will require them to seek for more loans and credit from the very same institutions which ultimately generates meaningful profits for them other than farmers. Although no one is opposing these businesses from making their profits, they shouldn't do it by claiming that they are involved in assisting developing farmers.

5. Lack of sustainability in established farmer support programs

As a commonly known fact, it is relatively easier to establish something when compared to the difficulty of maintaining or sustaining it. That's exactly what happens to some farmer support schemes that are meant to uplift developing farmers. In most cases, these programs and projects are initiated and operated by a combination of or a single institution. If the support that farmers get from their supporting programs does not show any sustainability, then it means that the farmers will also loose the chance of maintaining their supposedly improved status.

Note: Take note that the challenges mentioned in this chapter do not only highlight those that are experienced by developing farmers only, but they also include those that are experienced by each contributing role player. It goes without saying that by looking at the challenges that are experienced (or contributed) by farmers only will restrict the room for the transformation and growth of the industry. Since it's a combination of these challenges that retards the progress of the agricultural industry, it will equally be a solution of all these factors that will ensure the success of transforming previously disadvantaged farmers together with the success of Developing Agriculture.

9

STRATEGIES OF RESOLVING THE IDENTIFIED CHALLENGES

Given the string of challenges that create the setbacks that hinder the smooth operation of evolving this industry, it's quite inevitable that there would be a string of solutions that need to be derived. However, should these solutions be identified and applied in isolation to each other, the harmony of singing the song of farmer development may still be farfetched. It is important to note that identifying these solutions will only derive the melody of the song but may not necessarily confirm the harmony of it. So the best solution could be to develop a combination of problem solving techniques that will be able to enhance the chances of repairing the downfalls of success. This recommendation gives an indication that the best way to resolve the challenges of the industry would not be through the clichéd way of solving them one at a time, but through a combination of at least two methods that will allow problems to be resolved simultaneously. They are:

A. Derive a process that must be comprised of activities that will encompass the solutions of most problems.

A systematic procedure that will clearly be understood by farmers as well as their servants should be established. One of the best solutions that could see the industry succeeding in enriching its farmers and ultimately the economy lays in the establishment of a formalised route form that would allow farmers to grow from the point of being emerging farmers to fully developed farmers. On the other hand, this system will also serve as a guide to every agricultural role player in terms of determining when exactly they are supposed to provide their services and expertise to farmers. If applied and followed correctly, service providers of the industry will also be in a position of providing the most relevant services at the right time as opposed to the traditional practice of trying to assist farmers without assessing whether they've been to other relevant institutions prior to approaching the current service provider.

The system described above will aid in resolving various hiccups as follows:

- It will indicate the position of every agricultural institution in the sector
- It should help farmers know where to start looking for support and which route to follow onwards
- It will encourage collaborations amongst institutions
- It will aid in ensuring that each institution does not operate out of its area of speciality
- It will ensure that institutions involved in Developing Agriculture do not duplicate their work
- It will aid in reducing the turnover time of transforming these farmers

- It will surely expose role players who have a tendency of delaying their support to farmers

With this system in place, farmers will be familiar with the roles played by every institution that is meant to serve them. Starting with those who are within close proximity to them would be a good start. Farmers will often be spoilt for choice when it comes to the institution they prefer to choose for a specific service. The agricultural industry is one of the industries that have the luxury of having a number of institutions that can provide the same service. A very good example of this is that there are several fertilizer companies and research institutions that can analyse soil samples, and, there are quite a number of feed companies that produce and sell feeds of various farming enterprises. Therefore farmers will easily be able to choose their preferred service provider or supplier.

Diagram 6: The Protocol of Developing Agriculture (PDA) indicating each activity together with its responsible role player

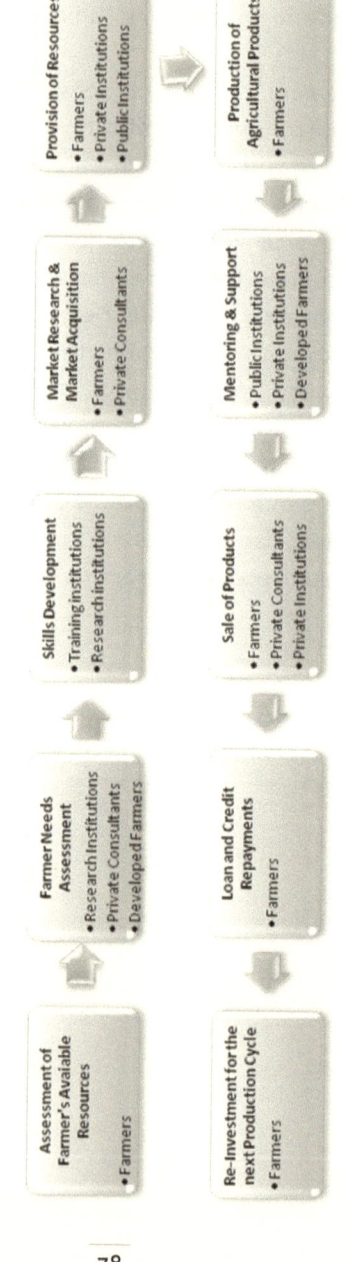

A scenario of the PDA System

Should this system be employed by the agricultural industry as a basic route form to be followed by every developing farmer, then every farmer and role player will know exactly what to do and most importantly when and by whom must it be done.

a) The activities of this system starts with a keen and committed farmer who needs to do an initial self-assessment to determine the most basic resources available to him/her; which could include land, skills, production inputs or even infrastructure. Identifying the available resources at this stage will assist in determining the best suitable enterprise to be pursued.

b) After acquiring the above information, the farmer will approach a trusted source; which will either be a research institution, a private consultant or better yet, a developed farmer for assistance in determining the developing farmer's most essential needs.

c) With all this in place, the farmer will then need to gather more or new skills that are adequate to his intended enterprise. This initiative must be taken by the farmer, although the skills will be provided by research and training institutions. Improved knowledge and skills will not only increase the farmer's competence but it will also boost his/her confidence of succeeding in the business.

d) As soon as the farmer has acquired sufficient skills and is in a well-informed position, he/she will now need to secure a market through market agents or by physically approaching potential clients. Marketing deals should preferably be formalised in writing to ensure that both parties keep to the agreement. In a case where farmers supply the informal market which is dominated by consumers and hawkers, then he/she will need to inform them in advance about the product intended to be produced. This will help the farmer to establish a client base which will go on to determine the farmer's scale of production. The information provided to potential clients should be as specific as possible and highlight the type of commodity to be produced, when it will be ready for sale, at which price, in what form etc. A good market research should also include a competitor analysis where the farmer will attempt to determine his/her competitors. This implies those who:

i) Produce the same commodity as the farmer intends to produce
ii) Are within close proximity to them
iii) Have the same target market

The collection of such information will play a role in determining the most suitable commodity to be produced, when will the market need it the most, in what quantities must it be supplied and at which prices will the market take them.

e) As soon as the decision on the enterprise is finalised, the skills are acquired and a market has been secured, it will then be the responsibility of the farmer to acquire the necessary resources that are relevant to the selected enterprise. These could be anything from funding, to infrastructure or production inputs. Some of these resources should be contributed by the farmers themselves, things like land, infrastructure or a proportion of the required capital. The farmer will approach any relevant stake holder for this activity. For instance funding will be sought for from banks and funding institutions, whilst production inputs can be provided by reputable input providers.

f) At this stage, the farmer will then be ready to start with his/her production. Production should take place with as much support as possible which must be provided from the time of putting the production plan together. This support must be sought from experienced mentors who understand the dynamics of the commodity to be produced. In most cases, its experienced farmers who are preferably not farming for themselves any longer who tend to make the best mentors because they don't view developing farmers as their immediate competitors.

g) Continuous monitoring together with the farmers commitment applied throughout the production period should yield good results (assuming that all the other production factors like climate were favourable). These will be reflected in the final harvest by means of maximised yields. The harvested products will then be sold by supplying and distributing the products according to the market agreement that has been entered into. In a case where the farmer supplies the informal market, he/she must reassure his customers of his supply in advance prior to supplying them as initially agreed or advertised. It is this activity that ensures the businesses income and profit.

h) Immediately after getting income from sales, the farmer must settle any debt that was acquired as a production resource. This refers to any loans or items acquired on credit.

i) Before the farmer makes any other financial commitments, money should be spared or saved as a reinvestment for the next production cycle.

Completing the first cycle of this system should occur with as much support and assistance as possible to farmers, thereafter, farmers should go through the next cycle with reduced assistance. The ability of the farmer to continue operating his farming business with reduced assistance will serve as an indicator of improvement. The activities of this system should be continuously reapplied until the farmer gains as much independence and experience as possible. Although some activities of the system may need to be eliminated with every progressive step made by the farmer, some of them will forever be practiced to encourage sustainability of the business. Examples of the activities that could be eliminated as the farmer progresses are, the development of particular skills, the provision of certain resources like production loans, once a good market relation has been formed the acquisition of a market can also be excluded in the next cycle. Whilst on the other hand, activities like mentoring and support, the actual production of products, selling of products and the reinvestment of the returns into the business will always need to be practiced.

The PDA system acts as a solution that encompasses some of the major problems that have been highlighted in the previous chapters.

B. Define the core additional solutions that are not included in the PDA

Even though the PDA system caters for some of the difficulties that are experienced in the industry, it doesn't cover the entire scope of challenges. Hence the following additional solutions have been defined.

I. Distinguish agricultural related matters from political matters

It's important to understand that although the industry took a knock from political events of the past regime, it must not be used as the battlefield to resolve such problems. Should problems that are not entirely agriculture based (even though they affect the agricultural industry) be given attention under the sphere of Developing Agriculture, then the main focus of finding the most relevant solutions will surely be shattered. Therefore the turnover time of transforming developing farmers and the industry will ultimately be prolonged.

II. Adaption of positive strategies that have been used in the past regime

The achievement of successfully commercialising the beneficiaries of the past era is actually an indication that some of the procedures and support systems that were applied back then were quite prosperous. The proof of this fact manifests in the vast number of sustainable farming operations that have been in existence across several generations. This suggests that some of the procedures and systems (only those that contributed towards the well-being of benefiting farmers) from the past should be adapted by the current regime.

III. Do away with restrictions on keen farmers

Since the major constraints of the industry started with oppression that restricted others from progressive support, it would be wiser to do exactly the opposite of that, which is to do away with restrictions on every keen farmer and provide every needy farmer with the relevant support. After all, it must be the well-being of the industry that takes priority and this can only be attained if no discriminatory practices are applied.

IV. True passion and commitment from farmers

A genuine and continuous passion for farming has already been identified as one of the foremost needs of every farmer. Having this as a prerequisite will serve as a solution in a sense that it aids in separating those who create negative statistics in the name of developing farmers when in actual fact they do not have the heart for farming. Farmers who possess the actual desire for farming will always see beyond any given challenge and will constantly strive to succeed. Such farmers will forever show appreciation for any form of assistance given to them by carefully nurturing it to ensure their business growth.

V. Reinvested contributions by successful farmers

The agricultural industry of South Africa should encourage developed and commercial farmers to reinvest their expertise in the development of the industry by sharing their experiences through mentorship programs as opposed to perceiving developing farmers as their future threats. The likelihoods of developed farmers to reduce their scale of production due to the growth of developing farmers are quite less since there is a continuous demand for agricultural products. If this is not reason enough, then the belief that the surface area used for agricultural purposes continues to be reduced should support the statement above. Productive farm lands and lands with good agricultural potential are mostly lost to developments such as housing. Therefore developing farmers shouldn't be viewed as threats to their mentors.

VI. Encourage competence amongst agricultural servants

The amount of competence required to provide farmers with the most relevant support is often neglected. Servants of the industry should take it upon themselves to gain as much competence as possible to ensure that they serve the industry accordingly. Newly graduated agriculturalists must develop a norm of understanding that high compatibility standards are compulsory in this industry and they cannot be compromised.

VII. Competence from agricultural institutions

Agricultural institutions that are involved in developing previously disadvantaged farmers should preferably be headed by a leadership that can concur with the position of these farmers. This could be those who were personally exposed to the same oppression, those who've worked in close contact with developing farmers over many years or even those who know exactly what it takes to succeed in the business of farming. Although experience in commercial farming would be a big boost, it's still not enough to constitute a good leader that would lead institutions of Developing Agriculture. The key issue is to have a leader that understands the mind set, perception and future prospects of developing farmers.

A combination of the above traits should form the scope of solutions that will see the industry succeed against the odds of the identified challenges.

10

CONCLUDING ON THE DEFINED VIEWS

It goes without saying that political motives of the past have greatly influenced the status quo of this industry, thus it's the very same politics that have the power to mend the problems that were born through it since all legislations and regulations are set at this level. However, all stake holders of the industry (including farmers) have the power to influence these regulations by indicating the direction in which the industry should be steered in. The direction in question entails creating favourable conditions and regulations that will see keen farmers progressing rapidly into fully-fledged commercial farmers, whilst enhancing the sustainability of commercialised farmers through the provision of relevant support and adequate services. By promoting the provision of such support services and encouraging idea sharing between farmers of different levels, there'll be a very strong chance of attaining a positive outcome that will benefit the individual farmer, the industry and eventually the economy. Perhaps these factors derive the key focus areas of Developing Agriculture which can be collated in a diagram.

Diagram 7: The focus areas of Developing Agriculture

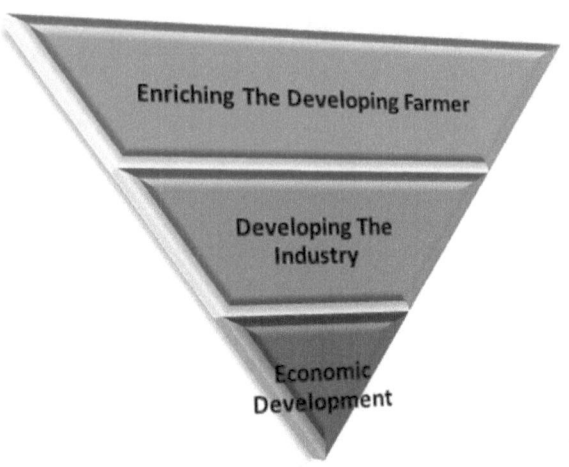

Even though the diagram above clearly illustrates that the ultimate goal of the agricultural industry is to contribute towards the growth of the local economy, it also indicates that this could be attained by concentrating on the building blocks that contribute towards it (the economic growth).

I.   Enriching the developing farmer

Developing farmers are the ones who most probably make up the majority as far as the scope of farmers is concerned. In addition to this, they have plenty of room for growth and development. Thus focusing on uplifting them will surely contribute towards growing the industry.

II. Development of the industry

The progress made by farmers symbolises the progress and growth of the industry. Similarly, the growth of the industry implies that greater contributions will be made towards the economy. One of the ways of measuring this focus area will be through monitoring the number of well-established farmers who were raised from the developing phase. A constant increase in this number will indicate the attainment of this focus area as well as the major objective of developing Agriculture.

III. Economic development

With agriculture being identified as one of the pillars of the economy, it can be declared that economic development rests on a well-managed and progressive agricultural sector amongst other sectors.

These focus areas will assist in ensuring that all efforts made by every role player are directed towards the same goal. However, this shouldn't create the implication that the future of the South African agricultural industry is totally out of focus, it simply suggests that the main focus or focus areas are not commonly known to many who are affected by them. Furthermore, it is also understood from previous chapters that the very same industry is contaminated by challenges that retards its growth and progress. Therefore awareness creation on the primary vision of the industry remains eminent and should also be a priority.

Based on the above stated connotations, it is evidently clear that the major constituents of success in the local agricultural industry will have to include every role player. Thus this proves beyond any reasonable doubt that although farmers are a part of the key components of Developing Agriculture, they are still not the sole contributors of success.

So then the conclusive implication on "The Roots of Developing Agriculture in The South African Context" is that the seed that should be planted by the industry is one that will encourage rapid growth and development on all the focus areas, and it should be nurtured by giving birth to systems and procedures that will promote progress, particularly amongst farmers.

REFERENCES

Crop Estimates Committee, 2004. www.daff.gov.za/cropestimates

Institute for poverty, land and Agrarian Studies, 2013. Smallholders and agro-food value chains in South Africa: Emerging practices, emerging challenges. Faculty of Economic and management Sciences, University of the Western Cape

South Africa.info, 2012. South African Agriculture. www.southafrica.info/business/economy/sectors/agricultural-sector

South Africa Yearbook, 2011/12. Agriculture, Forestry and Fisheries

Statistics South Africa, 2010. Concepts and Definitions for statistics South Africa, version 3. Statistics South Africa, Pretoria

Wikipedia, 2013. Liebig's Law of the Minimum. http://en.m.wikipedia.org/wiki/Liebieg's_law_of_the_minimum. (20 November 2013).